All About Animals
Gorillas

By Stephen Brewer

Reader's Digest Young Families

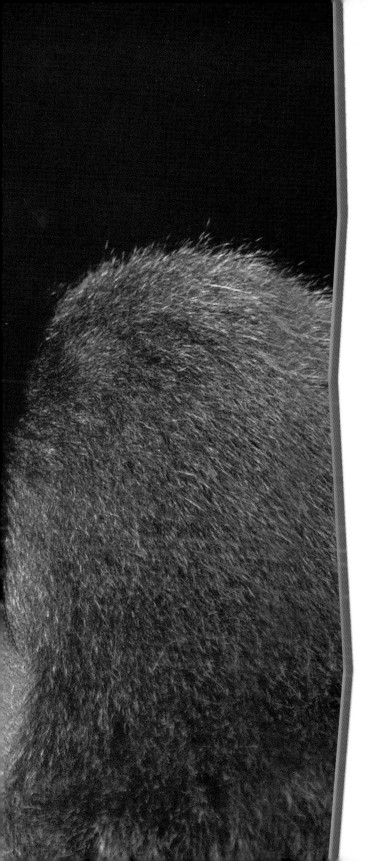

Contents

Chapter 1
A Gorilla's Day

Dawn is not a quiet time in the African jungle. It is filled with loud noises—screeching parrots, squealing monkeys, hooting chimpanzees, and other animals announcing the new day.

But the gorillas don't even seem to notice. They are sleeping in the soft nests they built from branches and leaves the night before. If any gorillas happen to wake up, they just lie there. They wait for the leader of their troop, a mighty male, to make the first move. Even the children who are cuddled up with their mothers don't get out of their nests, eager as they are to start playing. Their leader, called a silverback because his back is covered with silver-colored hair, makes all the decisions for his troop.

At last the 400-pound silverback climbs out of his nest. He stretches and yawns. He is hungry and ready for breakfast. The other fifteen gorillas, a mix of grown-up females and their children, are now allowed to leave their nests. The younger gorillas climb on their mothers' backs. The gorillas are ready to follow their leader. The troop soon comes to a thicket of young plants, and the gorillas feast on the tender shoots.

No Water for Me, Thanks
Gorillas don't drink water. They get all the liquid they need from eating plants.

Gorillas eat mostly plants, so they don't have to hunt or spend much time looking for food—the jungle is full of plants. So after breakfast, the gorillas bend back some tall grasses to make a soft place to lie down and stretch out while the little ones play.

The young gorillas climb, roll around on the ground, and crawl all over each other. Sometimes their mothers tickle them. The young ones even roughhouse with the grown-ups, who don't seem to mind at all.

Soon, all the gorillas are napping. When they wake up, they will move to another good place to eat and nap again!

The young gorillas stay with their family until they are eight years old. Then they leave the family. Most of the males will eventually become leaders of their own troop. The females will join other troops and start raising babies.

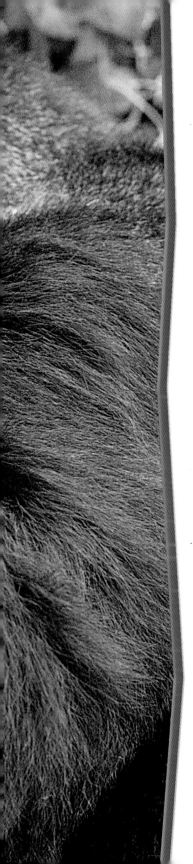

Just before sunset the gorillas eat dinner. The leader signals that it is time for the gorillas to build their nighttime nests. There are plenty of good plants around them. The mom gorillas groom their little ones, picking twigs and dirt out of their hair. They do the same for each other, and for the silverback leader, too.

Suddenly the low screech of a leopard is heard in the jungle. It is not far away! The silverback immediately stands on his hind legs and looks all around. He is over six feet tall and a very ferocious sight. It is his job to protect the gorillas in his family. He beats his chest very fast with his hands, stamps his feet on the ground, and lets out a few gigantic roars. Soon the sounds of the leopard's screeches fade away. The gorillas are safe. The little ones curl up with their moms, and all the gorillas go to sleep for the night.

Noseprints!

Gorillas can be identified by their noses! Like human fingerprints, no two gorilla noses are exactly the same. Scientists who work with gorillas often take close-up photographs of gorilla noses. These are called noseprints.

Chapter 2
The Body of a Gorilla

The hair along the backs of adult male gorillas begins to turn silver when they are twelve years old. Scientists call them silverbacks.

Big Hairy Apes

Gorillas are the largest primates, the group of animals that includes humans, monkeys, and other apes. Males weigh about 400 pounds and often stand more than 6 feet tall. Females are shorter, about 4½ feet tall, and weigh about 200 pounds—but that's still big!

Thick hair covers most of a gorilla's body, female and male alike. The hair is usually black and brown, but sometimes a gorilla will have reddish hair. The hair of gorillas that live high up in the mountains is thicker than the hair on gorillas living in lowland rain forests.

The only parts of a gorilla that are not hairy are the face, chest, fingers, palms, and the bottoms of the feet. These areas are covered with very thick black skin that protects the gorilla from the sharp thorns on plants.

When male gorillas reach adulthood—around the age of twelve—they develop broad, high foreheads, huge chests, and thick, shaggy hair on their arms. Looking so big and mighty comes in handy when a male is the leader of a gorilla troop and must defend it.

A Hairy Name

Gorillas are very hairy. That is why they are called gorillas. The word *gorilla* is from a Greek word that means "tribe of hairy women."

Walk Like a Gorilla

Gorillas walk on all fours and bend in their fingers. Only the knuckles of their third and fourth fingers touch the ground. By curling their fingers into their hands, gorillas protect them from injury. That's important because gorillas use their fingers to grab food, make nests, groom their hair, and to do other tasks.

Gorillas sometimes stand upright on their hind legs to reach fruit high on a tree or to get a better look around. Male gorillas stand on their hind legs to show off for females and to scare off strangers or predators.

Get a Grip

The big toes and thumbs of gorillas are opposite the other toes and thumbs, which lets gorillas grasp objects with both their hands and feet. Humans only have opposable thumbs so we can only use our hands for grasping.

At Arm's Length

The arms of gorillas are longer than their legs. This makes it easy to walk on all fours. Long arms also help when reaching for food.

Gorillas are called knuckle walkers because they walk on their knuckles.

Although gorillas are the biggest of the great apes, they are the quietest – except when a silverback is defending his troop or his mate.

Almost Human!

The gorilla is the second closest relative to humans. The closest is the chimpanzee. Like humans, gorillas have two arms and two legs, ten fingers and ten toes, ears on the sides of their heads, and thirty-two teeth. They can hear, see, smell, taste, and touch. Gorillas laugh, frown, get embarrassed, and show many of the same emotions we do.

Gorillas communicate by grunting, chuckling, roaring, screaming, growling, and making other sounds. Gorillas grunt when they are content and make high-pitched barks when they are curious. Silverbacks hoot and roar while beating their chests. Young gorillas hum, sing, and cry. Gorillas seem to have conversations by calling back and forth to one another.

Gorillas also use gestures and other signals to communicate. When a silverback wants the troop to move to a new location, he gets up and starts walking away while making soft sounds.

Some gorillas in captivity have learned to understand human language and to communicate with sign language.

Gorillas do not make tools, but they will grab a stick to knock fruit out of a tree or to measure the depth of water in a swamp before stepping in.

King of the Jungle

Over two hundred years ago, explorers came back from Africa with amazing tales of seeing hairy giants in the jungle. And no wonder! When a mighty male gorilla stands up on his hind legs, pounding his chest very fast, roaring loudly, and showing off his big teeth, he is one of the most frightening sights in nature. But male gorillas do this type of performance only to show off for females and to scare away intruders and rivals.

Despite their fierce shows of might, gorillas are really just very big bluffers! A male gorilla almost never attacks unless he is pushed into doing so by a stranger or rival. And when he charges toward another animal, usually another male gorilla, he often runs right past it or stops just short of touching it! Sometimes the two gorillas will stay face-to-face until one gives up and walks away.

Call of the Wild

When a male gorilla wants to show off his strength, he stands on his hind legs, roars, beats on his chest with open hands to make a loud *pok, pok, pok* sound, breaks off branches and shakes them at his rival, and even charges.

Despite their fearsome looks, gorillas are really shy, gentle creatures with peaceful ways. They are often called "gentle giants."

Chapter 3
Family Life

There can be as few as five or more than fifteen gorillas in a troop.

The Gorilla Troop

Gorillas live in a family group called a troop. Only one or two adult male gorillas are in each troop. One of them is the leader. He is always a silverback, easily identified by the silver hair on his back. All the gorillas in the troop accept him as their leader and follow him.

The leader makes all the decisions for the troop. He tells the other gorillas when to get out of bed, when to eat, where to go, and when to sleep. He also protects them from danger. He usually has an assistant, a male who is from eight to twelve years old and still too young to have his own troop.

The rest of the troop is made up of three or four adult females and their children. All the children are younger than eight years old. That's because most gorilla children are grown-up enough to leave the troop by the time they are eight. The females find an adult male and join his troop. Some males join all-male troops called "bachelor troops." Most male gorillas bond with females and form troops of their own. Once a female gorilla is a mom, she stays with the silverback and his troop for life.

Good Moms

A mother gorilla usually has three children in her lifetime, spaced about four years apart. She feeds and cradles her baby in her arms. When she walks on all fours, the baby rides on her back or clings, upside down, to her belly. By carrying the baby in these ways, the mother knows that her little gorilla is safe, and her arms are free for walking and gathering food.

Young gorillas ride on their moms' backs until they are about three years old. Then they romp through the jungle beside their mothers. The gorilla moms teach their little ones how to find food, build nests for sleeping, and stay out of danger. Young gorillas never stray too far from their mothers, and they share her nest until they are six years old.

Baby Gorillas

Newborn gorillas are tiny, weighing only 4 to 5 pounds. Average human babies weigh more—about 7 pounds. Gorilla babies grow quickly and are able to walk when they are $6\frac{1}{2}$ months old.

A mother gorilla spends almost all her time caring for her children.

Just like human kids, older gorilla children play with their younger brothers and sisters and help keep them safe.

Play Time

Young gorillas love to have fun. They play tag, king of the hill, and many other of the same games that human kids enjoy. They spend hours jumping in and out of trees. They even play catch with pieces of fruit!

Gorillas like to roughhouse, such as play-fighting with one another. The most fun of all, though, is jumping on the silverback who leads the troop and rolling all over him. He usually joins in the fun and tickles the young gorillas to make them squeal with delight.

All this playing isn't only for fun. It helps young gorillas learn how to get along with others. Since gorillas live in groups, this is important preparation for life.

Built-in Baby Monitor

Young gorillas who wander off to explore on their own can get into serious trouble, such as meeting up with a hungry leopard. But a young gorilla has a patch of white hair on its rump. This patch is called a tail tuft. The white tuft makes it easy for a gorilla mom to spot her child in the jungle.

Chapter 4
Eating and Sleeping

Gorillas use their hands to pick plants, peel stems and fruit, and dig into the ground for shoots and roots.

Big Eaters

Gorillas are mainly plant eaters. They eat all parts of plants—leaves, vines, fruits, flowers, seeds, stems, even bark and roots. Although gorillas eat 200 different kinds of plants, their favorites are bamboo trees, wild celery plants, and ginger plants.

Gorillas spend much of their day eating. They munch more than 40 pounds of plants a day! Gorillas have really big bellies. All the plant matter they eat causes their stomachs to expand!

Gorillas are not completely vegetarian. They also eat worms, ants, termites, and other insects that they scoop up with their hands.

Usually gorillas eat on the ground, but they do climb into low-lying branches and shimmy up trees to get fruit. But full-grown gorillas are too heavy to climb very high.

A Gorilla Picnic

When a gorilla troop comes upon a spot with tempting treats, the silverback may decide it is time for a picnic. The gorillas then make day nests out of grass and branches. They lie around for hours, munching and snoozing. They eat whatever food is within reach of their long arms. Sometimes this can add up to a feast!

Big Sleepers

Gorillas do not have one home. They build a new nest every night in a different place, even if the new place is near the old one. To make their soft nests, gorillas bend over branches or make a big pile of twigs and leaves. Sometimes female gorillas and their children sleep in the thick, low-lying branches of a bush or tree.

Wherever a silverback chooses for the troop to lie down, it is always in a place where food is close by. This means the gorillas don't have to go far to find food when they wake up—or even leave their nests if delicious plants can be reached without getting up! Snack time is all the time!

Gorillas spend a lot of time sleeping. They sleep about 12 or 13 hours each night. They also take naps during the day, including a long siesta in the early afternoon.

Rain doesn't seem to bother the gorilla's schedule of eating and sleeping. A gorilla's thick hair acts as a natural poncho, and the water runs right off the shaggy coat. Mountain gorillas, who live in rain forests at high altitudes, have especially long, thick hair. They don't even seem to notice a heavy rain.

Gorillas make soft, leafy nests during the day that they use for relaxing and sleeping. It's a good time for snuggling with Mom!

Chapter 5
Gorillas in the World

Where Gorillas Live

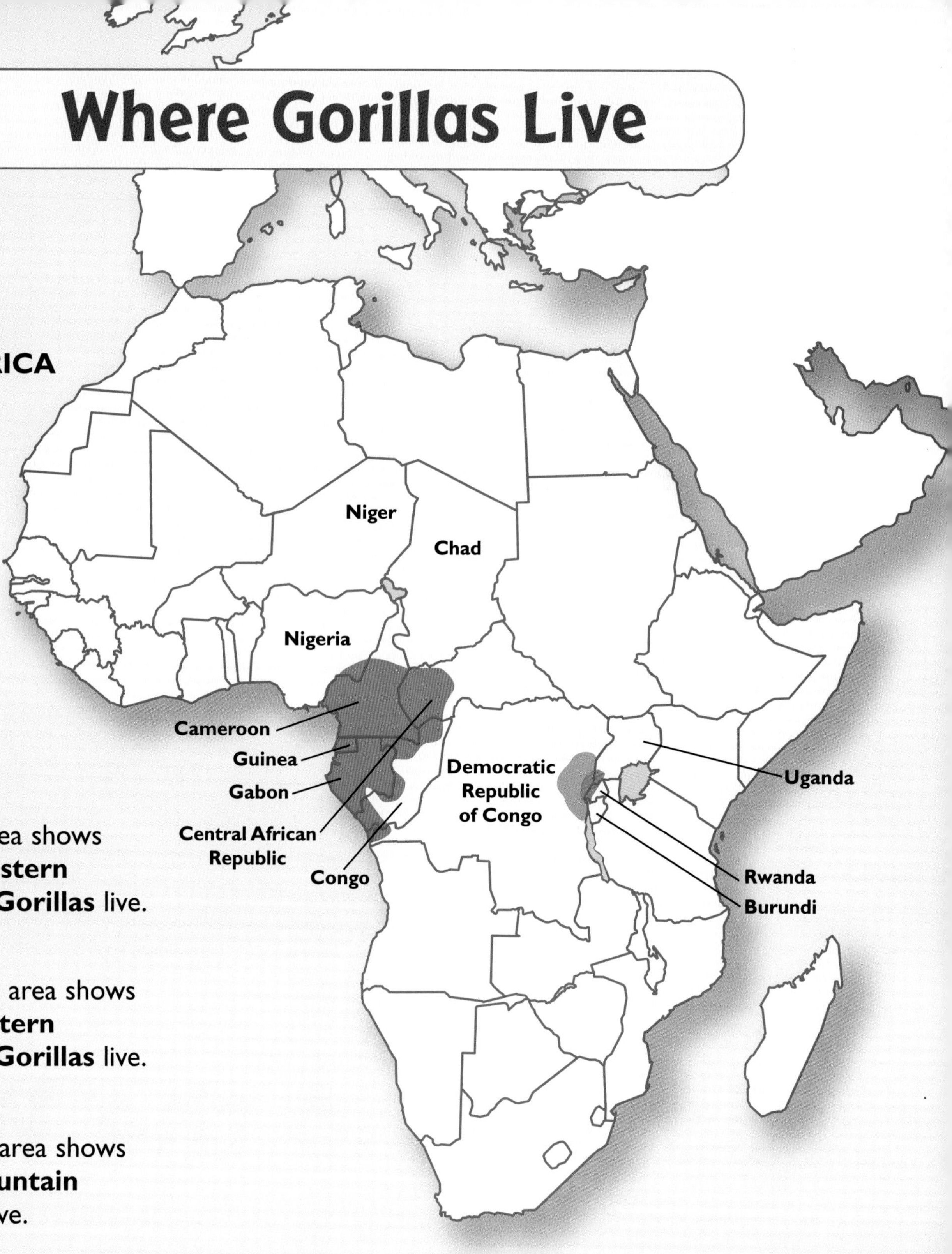

AFRICA

Niger

Chad

Nigeria

Cameroon

Guinea

Gabon

Central African
Republic

Congo

Democratic
Republic
of Congo

Uganda

Rwanda

Burundi

The red area shows
where **Western
Lowland Gorillas** live.

The purple area shows
where **Eastern
Lowland Gorillas** live.

The green area shows
where **Mountain
Gorillas** live.

Jungle Homes

Gorillas live in the wild in only one part of the world—in areas near the equator in Africa.

Most gorillas live in lowland jungles and swamps, and they are called Lowland Gorillas. The Western Lowland Gorilla has reddish hair and a very large brow ridge above its eyes. It makes its home in several countries in the western part of Africa. Most of the gorillas you see in zoos are Western Lowland Gorillas. The Eastern Lowland Gorilla lives only around the eastern part of the Democratic

Western Lowland Gorilla

Republic of Congo, which is in central Africa. It is larger than the Western Lowland Gorilla, and its hair is black and much longer.

Mountain Gorilla

A much smaller number of gorillas live in rain forests high up on mountains, and they are called Mountain Gorillas. They live at high altitudes, from 5,500 to 12,500 feet, in a small region that touches on Rwanda, Uganda, and the Democratic Republic of Congo. The Mountain Gorilla has a very thick coat of hair, which provides protection in the damp, cold weather at these heights. Scientists estimate that there are only 600 to 700 Mountain Gorillas in the wild today.

Saving the Gorillas

Gorillas have not been able to protect themselves from their worst enemies, humans. Scientists estimate that fewer than 100,000 gorillas are still alive. For many years, hunters killed these magnificent beasts and had them stuffed as prize trophies. People still hunt gorillas for their meat. Logging and land clearing are destroying much of the gorillas' habitat.

But some people are working hard to save gorillas. They provide food for people so they won't hunt gorillas. They hire guards to monitor illegal hunting and logging. And some nations have preserved gorilla habitats by creating national parks.

Fast Facts About Western Lowland Gorillas

Scientific name	*Gorilla gorilla*
Class	Mammals
Order	Primates
Size	Males up to 6 feet tall Females up to 5 feet tall
Weight	Males 400 pounds Females 200 pounds
Life span	About 35 years in the wild Up to 50 years in captivity
Habitat	Tropical rain forests, swamps

Famous Gorilla Friend

Dian Fossey, an American researcher, lived among Mountain Gorillas for more than twenty years. She earned the animals' trust by imitating their sounds and gestures. Much of what we know about gorillas comes from her. Today the Dian Fossey Gorilla Fund International continues her work to save these animals from extinction.

Glossary of Wild Words

bluffer   a pretender

edible   fit to be eaten

endangered   a species of plant or animal in danger of extinction

ferocious   very fierce and angry

groom   to clean the hair, skin, or fur by an animal

habitat   the natural environment where an animal or plant lives

knuckle walker   an animal that uses its knuckles for support when walking

predator   an animal that hunts and eats other animals to survive

Gorilla Stars

Some gorillas have become popular movie stars. The most famous of all is King Kong. Maybe you've also seen the movie *Tarzan*, about a boy raised by gorillas. These movies show us the true, tender nature of gorillas. King Kong, for example, looks scary, but he is kind and gentle at heart, and he's the hero you cheer for while watching the film.

primate mammals with a large brain and complex hands and feet, such as humans, apes, and monkeys

roughhouse to play roughly, possibly to the point of getting hurt/injured

siesta a Spanish word that means nap in the afternoon

silverback an adult male gorilla with silvery-colored hair on his back

tail tuft a small patch of white hair on the rump of a baby gorilla

terrestrial spends most of the time on the ground

troop a group of gorillas that live together

vegetarian an animal that eats only plants

Index